knitb

The basics & beyond

LANDAUER PUBLISHING, LLC

Copyright© 2015 by Landauer Publishing, LLC

This book was designed, produced, and published by Landauer Publishing, LLC
3100 101st Street, Urbandale, IA 50322
www.landauerpub.com / 515-287-2144 / 800-557-2144

President/Publisher: Jeramy Lanigan Landauer
Director of Operations: Kitty Jacobson
Project Manager: Janet Pittman
Technical Editor: Jane Townswick
Book Designer and Illustrator: Brian Shearer
Photographer: Dean Tanner, Primary Image Ltd.
Project Designers: Joyce Nordstrom
Janet Pittman

Special thanks to Nancy Wyatt,
Knitted Together, West Des Moines, IA for her
wonderful yarns and expert advice.

Library of Congress Control Number: 2014958396

This book printed on acid-free paper.
Printed in United States

10-9-8-7-6-5-4-3-2-1

ISBN 13: 978-1-935726-71-5

welcome to the
knitbook

In the past, women knitted out of necessity often gathering with others to share stories to the soothing rhythm of needles. Yesterday's necessity is today's pleasure. Today's knitting inspires with its variety of patterns and yarns both natural and synthetic in a dazzling array of colors, twists, weights and textures for projects ranging from art to funky and fashion.

Getting started takes just two simple stitches, knit and purl, and a ball of yarn to make a sensational scarf. Add a few simple techniques and you have a classic hat.

With the features-full **knit**book as your guide, you'll soon be knitting successfully and going beyond the basics to new techniques.

Knitters say there are no rules, so with the basics in hand, experiment. Get to know your yarns. Practice several of the stitch varieties offered. Explore, Enjoy. Celebrate and connect through knitting.

The Editors

Table of Contents

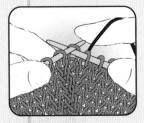

abbreviations

approx	approximately
B	Back. The side of the knitting not facing while knitting a row or a round
beg	beginning
BO	bind off
CO	cast on
cn	cable needle
dec(s)	decrease(s)
dpn(s)	double-pointed needle(s)
inc(s)	increase(s)
k	knit
kb	knit into the back of the stitch
kf	knit into the front of a stitch
kf&b	knit into the front and back of a stitch (inc)
k2tog	knit 2 stitches together (dec)
kwise	insert needle as if to knit
m1	make 1 (inc)
m1p	make 1 purl (inc)
p	purl
patt	pattern
pm	place marker
psso	pass slipped stitch over
p2tog	purl 2 stitches together (dec)
pwise	insert needle as if to purl
RS	right side

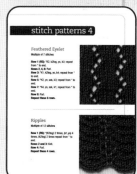

You'll experience immediate success as you learn new knitting techniques and stitches to complete each project.

getting started

knitbook, The basics & beyond is designed for the first-time knitter as well as those of you who want to brush up on your knitting techniques. For the novice, work from the front of the book, learning about knitting and the various stitches and techniques in a progression that combines stitch illustrations, practice stitch patterns, and colorful projects designed for each learning step along the way.

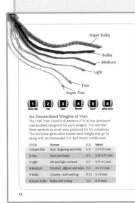

Gathering Yarn and Supplies shows many of the options available at yarn shops and craft stores. The charts and photographs explain the various weights, fiber content, and varieties of yarn available.

Photos and detailed explanations of supplies give you the knowledge to make great choices of yarn and equipment.

Knitting Basics gives you step-by-step illustrations of each part of the knitting process from making your first loop to finally removing the stitches from the needle. Photographs show how to fix mistakes and finish your pieces.

At the end of each section illustrating knitting stitches look for Stitch Patterns. Make a few

swatches of various stitch patterns for practice. You will find additional stitch samples in the Stitch Patterns Summary section.

Reading a Knitting Pattern includes the basic abbreviations used in knitting instructions and gives examples of the knitting shorthand used to describe the working process. The use of color and stitch charts is illustrated.

Going Beyond Basics shows you with step-by-step illustrations how to increase, decrease, and make stitches that add shape and texture to knitting. Photographs show special techniques and how to use some unique equipment.

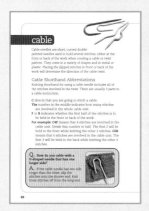

Working with Specialty Needles covers the use of circular and double-pointed needles which expands your techniques to include tubes, knitting in the round and knitting large projects. Using cable needles will give you another tool for adding texture and design to projects.

Finishing Touches gives you the extras that make your projects complete: fringe, tassels, buttons, and beads.

Gathering Yarn & Supplies

On the following pages, take time to get acquainted with what you'll need as you start on your adventures in knitting. Then, take a trip to your local knit shop or craft store and discover yarns in a dazzling array of colors, twists, weights and textures.

You'll be inspired to begin and have fun creating your own unique fashions and accessories.

yarn

Yarn is what makes a knitted project wonderful. There are natural and synthetic fibers in a variety of colors, twists, weights, and textures to choose from.

Natural fibers include wool, cotton, silk, and linen. Wool can come from various animals such as Shetland, lamb and merino (sheep); alpaca and angora (rabbit); and cashmere and mohair (goat). Wool is the most common fiber used for knitting, sometimes as a combination of 2 or more types of wool or in combination with another fiber. Some wool yarns are machine washable.

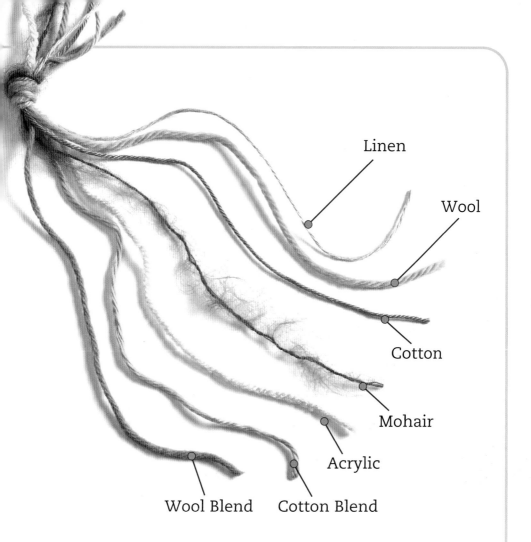

Linen

Wool

Cotton

Mohair

Acrylic

Wool Blend   Cotton Blend

Synthetic fibers include acrylic, polyester, and nylon made from petro-chemicals and acetate, rayon, and viscose made from wood pulp. Most synthetics are washable.

Yarns can be made all of one fiber, but there are many blends today that maximize the best of each fiber. A blend of natural and synthetic may be naturally soft, but have the hard-wearing, washable characteristics of the synthetic.

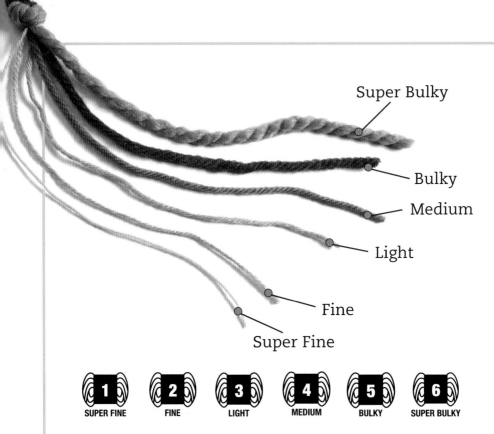

Six Standardized Weights of Yarn

The Craft Yarn Council of America (CYCA) has developed standardized categories for yarn weights. You will find these symbols on most yarn produced for US companies. The list below gives other names each weight may go by along with recommended U.S. and metric needle sizes.

CYCA	Names	U.S.	Metric
1 Super Fine	Sock, fingering and baby	1–3	2.0-3.25 mm
2 Fine	Sport and baby	3–5	3.25-3.75 mm
3 Light	DK and light worsted	5–7	3.75-4.5 mm
4 Medium	Worsted, afghan and Aran	7–9	4.5-5.5 mm
5 Bulky	Chunky, craft and rug	9–11	5.5-8 mm
6 Super Bulky	Bulky and roving	11+	8-10 mm

Twist

Most yarns are a twist of more than one ply or strand of yarn. Ply refers to the single strand of a fiber. Although some yarns (especially bulky) are single ply, more than 1 ply adds strength to the yarn.

Dye Lots

The yarn label is marked with a color number and a dye lot number (page 15). Always purchase enough yarn of one dye lot to make your project. A different dye lot number means that the yarn has been dyed in a different batch. There can be slight variations in color between dye lots and you would not want a visible line where you changed dye lots.

Yarns are given visual texture by adding variety in the dye. Variegated yarns have dye applied specific distances apart. Tweeds or heathered yarns are 2 or 3 plies of different colors or values twisted together.

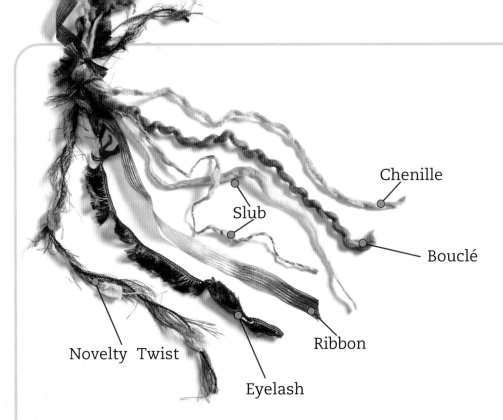

Chenille

Slub

Bouclé

Novelty Twist

Ribbon

Eyelash

Yarn Textures

Most of the projects in this book are knitted in a smooth twist yarn so you can see the pattern and learn the techniques easily. Then, you can have fun with some of these specialty yarns with different textures:

Chenille— A short piled yarn.

Bouclé—Formed from two yarns spun together at different speeds so one forms loops.

Slub—Thick and thin and usually loosely twisted.

Ribbon—A woven ribbon, soft enough to knit.

Eyelash—Resembles eyelashes and comes in a variety of "lash" lengths and thicknesses.

Novelty Twists—Two or more yarns twisted together and knitted as one yarn.

Reading Yarn Labels

The yarn label includes a variety of information about the yarn and how to use it. On the label below you will see the information available.

Fiber Content

Needle Size/
Stitch Gauge

Care Instructions

CYCA Weight
Number

Color

Dye Lot

There is some variation in labels on yarns produced for countries other than the United States. The label at right has most of the same information, except for the CYCA weight classification.

You can purchase yarn (clockwise from left) in unwound hanks, or center-pull round balls and oval skeins.

Rolling Hanks into Balls

Yarn that comes in a hank (above left) needs to be rolled into a ball for easy, even knitting.

When you purchase yarn as a hank at a yarn shop, you can probably get it rolled there with a yarn swift and ball roller. A yarn swift looks similar to a Ferris wheel and is adjustable. It turns around as the ball of yarn is wound, putting even tension on the yarn. Insert the yarn end from the hank into the ball roller and turn the crank handle. This gives you a pull ball like the green ball at right.

Q. How do you roll a ball from a hank if you don't have a swift and ball roller?

A. Undo the hank and have someone hold it around their upturned hands, with arms spread to put slight tension on the yarn or slip it over a chair back. Make a notch at one end of a shortened empty tube from a paper towel. Insert the yarn end in the notch. Wrap the yarn around the tube, rotating the tube as you wind until all of the yarn is wound into a ball. Use the yarn in the notch as a center pull.

Choosing Yarn for Your Project

Probably the easiest way to choose yarn is to select a project; then select a yarn in the suggested weight category. If you find a yarn you love, first try to find a corresponding project pattern.

If you cannot find a pattern you like for that yarn weight, knit gauge samples (pages 42-43) with the suggested needle size and one larger and smaller. Then, see if you can find a pattern in one of these gauges where a few adjustments can easily be made. Your yarn shop may be able to help with these adjustments.

Using Novelty Yarns

There are many fun novelty yarns to choose from. You can make a whole project with novelty yarns or combine them with another novelty or plain yarn (see right).

Consider the fiber content and care requirements in combining yarns. For a scarf which may need little cleaning this will not be as important as a novelty yarn used in a sweater.

When using two yarns together you may need to use a larger needle. First make a gauge sample (page 42) using the larger of the two recommended sizes. If the sample is too firm, knit a gauge with a larger needle. Frequently a lightweight novelty yarn knits in with another yarn without a need to increase to the needle size.

Photos from top: Polyester long eyelash/fun fur, nylon slub, and nylon/polyester novelty yarns knitted together with the same medium-weight lavender acrylic yarn.

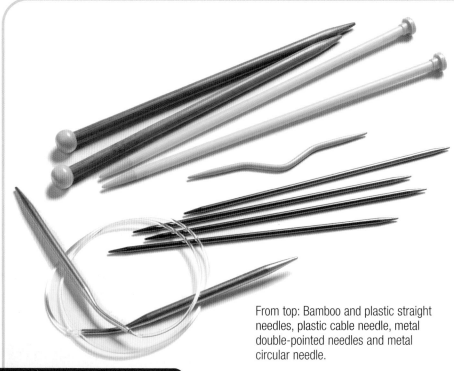

From top: Bamboo and plastic straight needles, plastic cable needle, metal double-pointed needles and metal circular needle.

needles

There are several characteristics of needles to consider in knitting: *size* which is the diameter of the needle, the *material* it is constructed from, *length*, and *shape*.

Size of the needle determines the size of your stitches. Size numbers get larger as the diameter of the needle increases. This size will make a difference in the gauge of the stitches (page 42). Many knitting needles are designated with both a U.S. size (a number) and a metric size (the actual diameter of the needle) which is used in the rest of the world. (See chart, page 12.)

Generally you use a smaller needle for knitting with thin yarn and a larger needle for thicker yarn. Made with the same yarn, the knitting on a small needle will be dense and firm while on a large needle, it will be lacy and loose.

Material determines the hand feel and yarn mobility of the needle. Needles come in several materials: wood and bamboo, plastic and metal. Each type of material has special characteristics.

Metal needles are slippery and inflexible. This makes them faster for knitting with some yarns because there is no drag of yarn against the metal.

Wood, bamboo, and plastic needles tend to be more flexible and, although smooth, may not be as slippery. These are better choices for beginning knitters and intricate stitch projects, such as cable patterns.

Length is determined by the project you are knitting. An extra-long straight needle will make knitting cumbersome and a too short needle will bunch up the stitches and make control of the knitting difficult. There are three standard lengths for straight needles (10", 12", and 14"). Choose the length that will hold your stitches without bunching them together. For very large projects, many knitters prefer to use circular needles or the flexible style of straight needle.

The shape of the tip can be sharp or rounded. A sharp tip can split some yarns, but makes knitting with a tight gauge easier. A blunt or more rounded tip may be harder to pick stitches but is easier to use on bulky or loose twist yarns. Sample both and choose what is best for your style of knitting and the yarn you are using.

Besides the tip characteristics of a needle, your project will dictate if you want to use straight needles, circular needles or double-pointed needles.

Straight needles

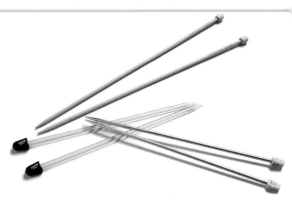

(right) come in several lengths and are used to make flat knitting such as scarves, blankets and the parts of some sweaters. They come in pairs and have a point at one end and a stop at the other end. Knitting is done from one needle to the other, turned and worked back in the other direction.

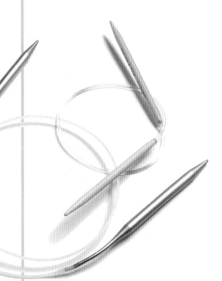

Circular needles (left) are two

short needles that are connected by narrow flexible nylon or plastic tubing. The total length varies from 12" to 60". They can be used to knit a large seamless tube for a sweater or hat. Many times they are also used for large flat projects or in place of straight needles. Some circular needles have very flexible tubing. Pictured at left are metal and bamboo circular needles. For special instructions, see pages 84-85.

Flexible needles look like

circular needles that have been cut in two with a stop at the flexible end. They come in several lengths and are used in place of straight needles. Because they are flexible except for the first 6" they are easier to use in a tight working situation, such as an airplane and are easier to pack and carry.

Double-pointed needles have points on both ends. They come in a set of 4 or 5 matching needles. They are used to make narrow tubes such as socks, mittens, and leggings. Pictured below are bamboo double-pointed needles. For special instructions, see pages 86-87.

Cable needles are short, frequently curved double-pointed needles used to hold several stitches when creating a cable pattern. Pictured at right are various shapes of metal and plastic cable needles. For special instructions, see pages 88-89.

Needle Gauge

A needle gauge has holes for inserting needles to check the size. (The size is marked on most needles, but sometimes the mark is hard to read or wears off.) Some gauges also have a ruler for measuring the stitches and rows per inch.

other supplies

1. Tape Measure
For measuring your project.

2. Crochet Hook
Keep a few sizes of crochet hooks around for helping to fix minor mistakes and for making some edge finishes.

3. Sewing Needles
A tapestry needle has a large eye and a rounded point. It is used to weave in yarn ends and to stitch seams together. Made especially for knitters are tapestry needles with a bent tip for weaving in and out of knit loops.

4. Point Protectors

Use these rubber or plastic caps on the tip of your needles to prevent the stitches from slipping off.

5. Place Markers

A place marker is slipped on the needle as directed in a pattern. The marker is slipped from one needle to the next and not knitted into the work. Some markers open and close, so you can use them around a stitch or around the needle.

6. Small Scissors

Don't be tempted to try to break yarns. This will stretch the fibers and some yarns may cut your hands before they break.

7. Row Counter

Especially useful for more detailed stitch patterns. Change tally at the end of each row.

8. Long Pins

Long pins are useful for holding two parts of a project together for stitching seams. The large flat head on some pins helps keep it from slipping through the loops of the knitting.

9. Stitch Holders

A stitch holder temporarily holds stitches while you knit another part of the project. See page 79 for a stitch holder in use.

> **Q:** How do I store and keep track of my needles?
>
> **A:** Purchase or make a cloth case with pockets for your straight needles; place circular needles in plastic sleeves or bags, being sure not to kink the tubing; and keep sets of double-pointed needles together with a rubber band. Or, place all of your needles in a plastic box with a tight lid. Keep a list of your needle sizes and shapes in a vinyl pouch in this book. Update the list each time you make a purchase.

Knitting
Basics

Now that you know about yarn and
supplies, let's begin to knit. On the
following pages, you'll find the step-
by-step instructions and easy-to-
follow illustrations for learning to
Cast On, Knit, Purl and Bind Off.
You'll soon be saying, "I made this."

knit & purl

From the knit and purl stitches you will be learning, you can make a variety of basic stitch patterns. The most common are garter, stockinette, seed or moss, and ribbing. All other stitch patterns are also a combination of these two stitches with the addition of increases, decreases, cables and open work.

Garter Stitch

If you make all of the stitches (rows) in a project with the knit stitch (or the purl stitch) the pattern is called garter stitch. This is a flat, dense knit that resists curling and has stretch in both directions. There are loops on both sides.

Stockinette

Stockinette stitch (knit one row and purl one row) is what we see most often in purchased garments. It has more stretch widthwise and unless blocked (page 49) it will curl on the edges. All of the loops are on one side, usually the wrong side. The photograph above left shows the stockinette stitch (smooth side up). The photograph at right is the back of the stockinette stitch. Sometimes a pattern will call for "reverse stockinette" which makes the loop side of stockinette the right side.

Seed or Moss Stitch

The seed or moss stitch is a combination of alternating knit and purl stitches. Frequently they are stitched with an uneven number of stitches per row. Knit 1, purl 1 across the first row, ending with a knit 1.

Keep this pattern across the rows and for all rows. If you have an even number of stitches, Row 1 is knit 1, purl 1 across and Row 2 is purl 1, knit 1 across. This pattern has alternating loops. The seed stitch is frequently used on the edges of projects because it does not roll like the stockinette stitch.

Ribbing

Ribbing is a combination of knit and purl stitches. At left above, knit 1, purl 1 ribbing is worked similar to the seed stitch above except that the direction of the loop is always the same. The ribbing at right above is knit 2, purl 2. Ribbing can be stitched in multiples of 1, 2, 3, or more groups of each stitch.

Ribbing has more crosswise stretch than most patterns and is frequently found at the bottom, sleeve and neck edges of sweaters, the bottom of mittens and hats, and at the top edge of socks. Sometimes instructions will call for using 1 size smaller needle to knit the ribbing.

needle & yarn basics

To Get Started

Select a pair of 10" or 12"-long straight needles and a worsted-weight (CYCA #4) yarn in wool, wool blend, or acrylic.

Sit in a comfortable chair with no arms; pull it back slightly from a table where you can set this book.

Other equipment you need for learning the basics are a ruler, measuring tape, or other gauge measure (page 42) and a pair of small scissors. As you proceed through the book there will be other equipment you will want to have.

Starting on the next page read the instructions and look at each section of illustrations. With your needles and yarn, work along practicing each section. Most illustrations have the yarn for the current step highlighted in magenta.

Basic Vocabulary

Ball Yarn: The yarn that is connected to the ball or skein you are working from.

Working Yarn: The yarn you are knitting with at that time.

Tail End: The end of the yarn opposite the ball or skein.

Slip Knot: The knot made to start your knitting.

Cast On: Putting a row of stitches on the needle to start your project, page 32.

Bind Off: Taking stitches off at the end of a knitted piece or when shaping some pieces, page 40.

Row: One time working across the stitches on a needle.

knitting styles

English, American, or Right-hand Carry Method

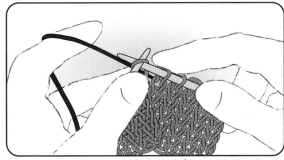

Continental or Left-hand Carry Method

There are two main styles of knitting, the English (American) and the Continental. The formation of the stitches is the same but the method of holding the working yarn is different.

English Method: The working yarn is drawn through your right-hand fingers and wrapped around the right needle with the right hand. This is frequently called the "throw" method. All illustrations in **knit**book show the English method.

Continental Method: The working yarn is drawn through the left-hand fingers and right-handers use the right needle to loop around the working yarn. This is frequently called the "pick" method. A left-hander may use the left index finger to wrap the working yarn around the right needle.

getting started

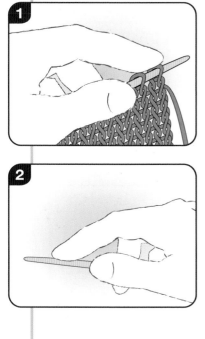

Holding the Needles

The knitting process is the same for both right and left handers. At the start of a row the left needle has all of the stitches on it. Hold this needle with your thumb parallel along the needle, the index finger resting on top near the tip and the remaining fingers slightly curved and supporting the needle and the already knit work.

Hold the empty right needle with your thumb parallel to it with your index finger resting on top near the tip and the remaining fingers slightly curved and supporting the needle; the knitted work will pass from the left needle to the right needle as you knit.

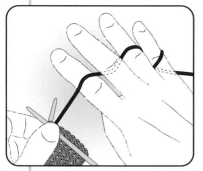

Holding the Ball Yarn

For the English or right-hand carry method, start wrapping the yarn around your right hand near the last stitch knitted. Wrap the yarn around the little finger, over the ring finger, under the middle finger and over the index finger. Gradually move the hand away from the stitching until the tension is firm but loose enough to form stitches. Or, you may hold the working yarn between your right thumb and index finger.

slip knot

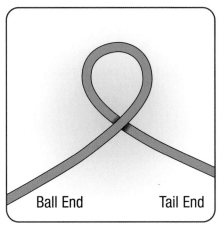

1. Form a crossover loop with the tail end on the bottom and the ball end on top.

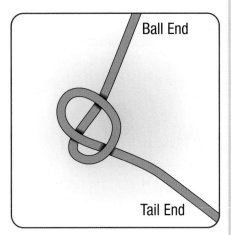

2. Carry the ball end under the loop.

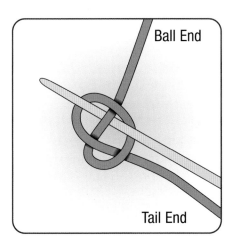

3. Insert the proper size needle over the bottom of the original loop, under the lower yarn and over the top of the original loop.

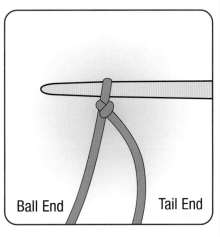

4. Pull the ends of both yarns to tighten. This slip knot forms the first stitch.

cast on

The first step in knitting is to put stitches on the needle. This is called casting on. We are showing you two basic methods. Long tail cast on and E or loop cast on. Both begin with a slip knot (page 31).

Long Tail Cast On

This method gets its name from the long tail of yarn you need to pull from the ball before making your slip knot for the first stitch. Leave a tail about 3 times the width of the project you are casting on or about 3/4" for each stitch. Long tail cast on is a firm cast on that appears to already have one row of knitting finished.

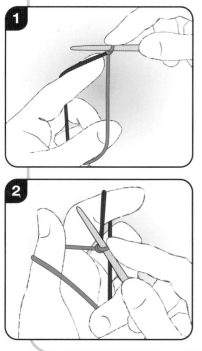

Use one needle for casting on. Leaving a long tail, make a slip knot (page 31) in the yarn and place it near the tip of the needle. Hold the needle in your right hand. Position the long tail end (lavender) to the front and the ball end (magenta) to the back. Insert thumb and index finger of left hand between the yarns. Hold both tails in your palm secured loosely with your other fingers.

Spread your thumb and index finger apart and let the long tail end (lavender) wrap around your left thumb and the ball end (magenta) wrap over your index finger. Continue to hold the tails in your palm, secured loosely with your fingers.

Insert the needle under the front thumb loop.

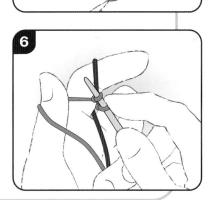

Move the needle over the ball yarn and pull it under the thumb yarn.

Pass the thumb loop over the tip of the needle, letting the loop slide off the end of the thumb. Tighten the new loop (second stitch) on the needle.

Pick up the left yarn around your left thumb as in 1 at left and repeat, forming loops (stitches) on the needle until you have the required number of stitches.

Loop (E) Cast On

The Loop cast on gets its name from the simple loop you make on the needle. As you are pulling the loop snug the yarn looks like an "E" so sometimes it is called the E cast on. This method can also be used to add stitches at the end of a row. Care must be taken when knitting the first row because it is easy to drop the cast on. This cast on forms a soft loose edge.

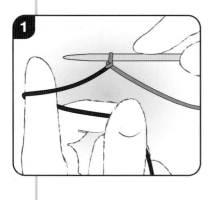

Start with a slip knot (page 31) several inches from the end of the yarn (no need to measure here). Hold the ball yarn (magenta) in your left hand wrapped from front to back around your index finger and held between your thumb and middle finger.

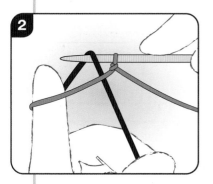

With the point of the needle, wrap around the working end of the yarn from right to left (back to front).

Let the yarn slip off your index finger leaving the loop on the needle.

Snug the working yarn. Pick the working yarn up over your index finger and repeat forming loops on the needle until you have the required number of stitches.

Q. **What are the differences between Long Tail Cast On and Loop Cast On?**

A. The Long Tail Cast On makes a firm edge along the bottom of the knit piece and each cast on is a completely formed stitch.

The Loop or E Cast On makes a looser edge that you might want to use for a shawl or throw, or a garment that has a soft edge. Because you do not have to leave a long tail, it works well for projects with a large number of stitches. The main drawback of a Loop Cast On is that a knotted stitch is not formed, making it easy to drop a stitch when working the first row.

knit stitch

In knitting there are 2 basic stitches, knit and purl. Used in various combinations these two stitches make many patterns.

When completed each knit stitch makes a smooth stitch on the side you are working on and forms a loop (bump) on the opposite side. The following illustrations have the yarn for the current step highlighted in magenta.

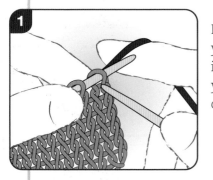

Hold the needle with the stitches in your left hand and the empty needle in your right hand. Place the working yarn (from the ball or skein) in back of the needles.

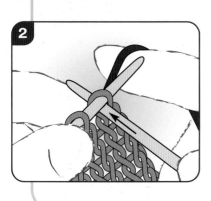

Insert the tip of the right needle into the first stitch from left to right.

While holding the right needle with the tip of your left thumb and index finger, use your right hand to pass the yarn behind and over the right needle.

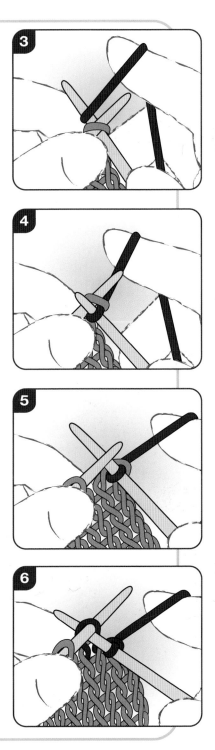

Pushing with your left index finger and using your right hand to rotate the right needle, bring the tip of the right needle with the loop of yarn through the original stitch.

Push the original stitch up and off the left needle.

Gently tighten the working yarn on the right needle if necessary to complete the first stitch.

Repeat steps 1 through 5 across the stitches on the left needle, putting the new row of stitches on the right needle.

purl stitch

The purl stitch is the opposite of the knit stitch, making a loop (bump) on the front of the work and is smooth on the back. Once stitched and removed from the needles, you cannot tell the difference in a knit and purl stitch.

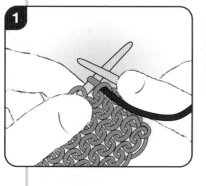

1

Hold the needle with the stitches in your left hand and the empty needle in your right hand. Place the working yarn in front of the needles.

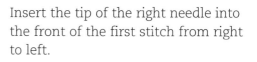

2

Insert the tip of the right needle into the front of the first stitch from right to left.

While holding the right needle with the tip of your left thumb and index finger, use your right hand to pass the yarn around the right needle and between the needles from right to left.

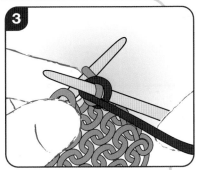

Using your right hand, slide the right needle down, bringing the tip of the right needle with the loop of yarn through the stitch and away from the front.

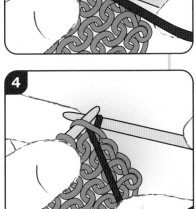

Push the original stitch up and off the left needle. Gently tighten the working yarn on the right needle if necessary to complete the first stitch.

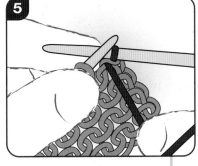

Repeat across the stitches on the left needle putting the new row of stitches on the right needle.

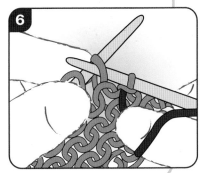

bind off

Most of the time you will be instructed to bind off at the end of a piece. Or, you may be instructed to bind off a few stitches at the beginning or in the middle of a row.

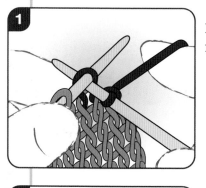

Knit 2 stitches onto the right needle.

Insert the tip of the left needle from left to right into the front of the far right stitch on the right needle.

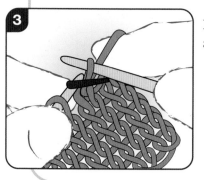

Lift this stitch over the second stitch and the tip of the right needle.

Knit the next stitch from the left to the right needle. Repeat steps 2 and 3, lifting the far right stitch up and over the second stitch. Continue until there is only one stitch left.

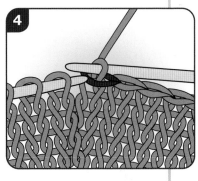

Cut the working yarn leaving about a 6" tail. Enlarge the loop of the last stitch, pull the yarn tail through and tighten.

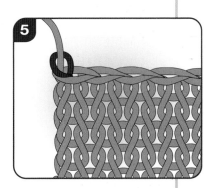

Q. **How do I bind off in purl stitch or a pattern of knit and purl?**

A. To bind off in purl stitch, purl 2 stitches. Insert the tip of the left needle into the front of the far right stitch on the right needle from left to right, lifting it over the second stitch and the tip of the needle. If you are working a pattern of knit and purl stitches, follow that pattern as you work stitches onto the right needle.

![A variety of tools for measuring your stitch gauge.]

A variety of tools for measuring your stitch gauge.

gauge

A stitch gauge is given at the beginning of every project pattern. This gauge is used to determine the width and length of a project piece. Make a test sample with the yarn you have selected and the suggested needle size to determine your gauge. Knit this test in stockinette stitch (knit one row and purl one row) or in the stitch pattern indicated in your pattern.

Cast on 4 times the suggested number of stitches per inch. For example: if the gauge states 5 stitches per inch with size 6 needles, cast on 20 stitches (4 x 5). Knit in stockinette stitch until the swatch measures 4". Now measure the number of stitches in 1" as directed in the photos below.

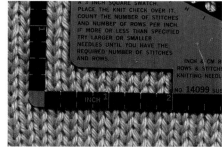

Check the gauge by measuring 1", placing long pins at that distance, and counting the number of stitches (4½). Or use a purchased gauge that has a cut out to help with the measuring and counting.

These samples were knit with the same yarn using 3 different sizes of needles. At left, size 5, center, size 9, right size, 10½. You can see that the stitches have gotten bigger, making the swatch and the gauge larger.

Counting the stitches

One stitch is the single upside down vase-shaped loop formed by either knitting or purling. One knit stitch is highlighted at right in purple. If the gauge includes a half stitch you would count just one side of the stitch.

Changing the Gauge

If the swatch you have made does not have the same gauge as called for in the pattern, change needles and knit another sample. If there are more stitches to the inch in your sample, use the next size larger needles. If there are fewer stitches to the inch in your sample, use the next size smaller needles. An exact gauge is important as you start making sweaters and other projects that must be a certain size.

The number of rows per inch is sometimes given as part of the gauge. This number is not as important as the number of stitches per inch. Most patterns indicate how many inches in length to make a piece rather than how many rows to work.

Changing Yarn

Changing yarns from the one called for in the project instructions can also change the gauge. Yarns given a CYCA number (page 12) will knit with about the same gauge. But because there are differences in yarns and there are differences in how you might knit each yarn, you may still need to make some adjustments in needles.

special techniques

Adding a New Ball of Yarn

It is best to add a new ball of yarn or change colors at the beginning of a row. Leaving a 6" tail from the new ball knit a few stitches. Make a loose knot with the tails of the new and the old yarn. Adjust the loop size of the new stitches and continue stitching with the new yarn.

You can add a new ball of yarn in the middle of a row, but it may leave a knot on the surface of your work. On a scarf or other reversible project, the knot may show.

Weaving in Yarn Ends

After finishing a knit piece, you will have yarn ends or tails from the casting on and binding off processes, from adding a new ball of yarn, and/or from changing yarn colors.

New Yarn on Edges

After your piece is finished, tighten any loose knots. Thread the tail into a tapestry needle. Use the threaded needle to weave the tail through the knitting loops. Weave in about 3", pull through and snip yarn. If you have more than one color of yarn, weave the tail into the same color.

New Yarn in Middle of Row

For new yarn added in the middle of a row, thread a tapestry needle and individually weave each end through the loops of the knitting. If the pattern is garter stitch or stockinette stitch, you can weave the yarns diagonally or along a row. If the yarn color matches you can also weave yarn tails from the edges into the piece diagonally.

Yarn from Cast On and Bind Off

At the beginning and end of a knit piece, you will have a tail of yarn. After your piece is finished, thread the tail into a tapestry needle. Use the threaded needle to weave the tail through the knitting loops along the bottom or top edge. Weave in about 3", pull through and snip yarn.

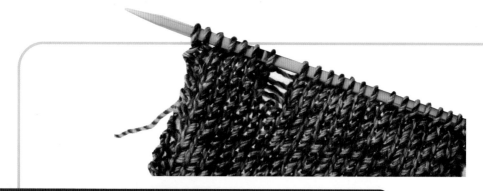

correcting mistakes

Even the most accomplished knitters make mistakes once in a while. The most common mistakes are split yarn and a dropped stitch. Try to fix a mistake as soon as possible.

A Mistake in the Current Row

To get to the mistake (here a split yarn on the 4th stitch on the right needle), unravel one stitch at a time from the right needle by inserting the left needle in the loop of the row directly under the current stitch.

Carefully slide the current stitch up and off the tip of the right needle, releasing the yarn. Leave the stitch from the previous row on the left needle, making sure the stitch is not twisted. Repeat these steps until you have unraveled the mistake; resume knitting.

Dropped Stitches Within a Few Rows

If the stitch has only dropped a row or two, use one of the knitting needles to pick up the loop of the stitch. Pull it up and over the bar of yarn in the row above, turning the needle to pick up the bar. Work your way back up to the current row.

Dropped Stitches Down Several Rows

If there is a long ladder above the dropped stitch, use a crochet hook to pick up the strands of yarn.

For a knit stitch, insert the crochet hook through the loop from front to back and under the bar of yarn above it.

Pull the bar through the loop. This is the new loop. Repeat at each bar of the ladder until you are at the top. Put the final loop on the left needle and knit it. Continue working across the row.

Correcting Dropped Purl Stitches

If the dropped stitch is a purl stitch, turn the piece over and correct as above for a knit stitch.

Q. What is a split yarn?

A. With some yarns of more than one ply, it is easy to split the yarn with the tip of the needle as you are making a stitch. If you have a split yarn, correct it with one of the methods in this section.

Correcting A Mistake Many Rows Back

If you discover a mistake several rows back, especially if you have an intricate stitch pattern, mark the mistake with a place marker that opens (shown here) or a piece of a different color of yarn, so you know which row the mistake is in.

Remove the project from the needle and carefully pull the working yarn to unravel the knitting, stopping one row above the mistake. Place the stitches on a needle with the working yarn going on last (shown here). Now unravel one stitch at a time, referring to A Mistake in the Current Row (page 46) being sure to pick up the stitches so they are not twisted. Stop when you have unstitched the mistake and resume knitting.

Q. **Which way do I stitch when I pick my knitting up?**

A. When possible, stop knitting at the end of a row. If you stop in the middle of a row you must be very careful to restart in the correct direction with the working yarn connected to the knitting on the right-hand needle.

blocking

Most knitting projects need to be blocked to make the piece lay flat and conform to the size stated in the directions. This will be important when you knit garments.

Place each piece individually on a large, flat, padded surface. For many projects, an ironing board will work. Or, you can lay a folded cotton towel or heat-resistant blanket on a heat-proof surface and cover with a cotton sheet.

Place the knitted piece wrong side up on the prepared surface. Pin to the padding with steel pins, stretching, easing, and smoothing as necessary, into the stated measurements. Use a tape measure for accuracy. Place pins about an inch apart around the piece to make straight edges.

For cotton and wool, dampen a light-weight cloth. Lay it over the pinned piece. Press lightly, using a straight-up-and-down motion with a warm iron. Do not set the full weight of the iron on the piece or move the iron back and forth because this will flatten the texture of the stitches. To use a steam iron, hold it over but do not touch the pinned piece. Dry completely before removing pins and blocking the next piece. For synthetic fibers, refer to yarn label instructions.

For ribbing, pin without stretching. Steam but do not press the ribbing on the edge of a piece.

joining pieces

After all of your pieces are blocked, it is time to sew them together. Use a tapestry needle or one especially designed for this purpose (page 22). Thread the needle with matching yarn. (These photographs feature burgundy yarn to highlight the stitches.)

Securing the Start

Use a piece of the knitting yarn no more than 18" long. Starting about 3" above the bottom, weave the yarn down the side edge of one piece of the knitting to the bottom.

Place the pieces to be joined on a flat surface with the edges next to each other, right sides up, matching the bottom and top edges. As you work, sew the edges together row by row. Bring the yarn from the back to the front through the space between the first and second stitches in the bottom row and then from front to back through the corresponding space on the other piece. Pull snugly to join the bottom edge.

Joining Pieces–Ladder Stitch

Joining Side Edges

To join two pieces along the side edges, match the ends and secure. Then, weave the two edges together, catching the strand between the first and second stitch on each side carrying the thread on the front of the seam. The sewing yarn will appear as a ladder, with the strands going crosswise between the two pieces. Pull firmly as you go up the seam. This seam will be hidden.

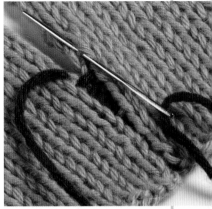

Joining Bound-Off Edges

For two cast off edges, lay the pieces on a flat surface, butting the edges together and matching the ends. Secure the right edges to start. Working the ladder stitch, as described above, weave in and out, catching two strands of the last row of stitches before the cast off. Go in the space where you came out on the previous stitch. Pull the yarn to form what appears to be another row of knitting. The cast off portions will roll to the back.

> **Q.** Should I stitch my project together with my knitting yarn, even if it seems to fray easily?
>
> **A.** Use 12" lengths of yarn so they will not be pulled through the knitting as many times as 18" lengths. If your yarn is not very strong, is highly textured, or is bulky, use a matching color and weight of worsted yarn.

Joining Cast-Off and Side Edges

To join a cast-off edge to a side edge, lay the pieces together flat, right sides up. Secure the right edges to start. Work through the cast-off edge, catching two strands of the last row of stitches before the cast off and catching the strand between the first and second stitch on the side edge. Pull firmly as you go up the seam.

Joining Pieces–Backstitch Seam

Instead of using a ladder stitch, you can position the pieces on top of each other and stitch a more conventional-looking seam. For this type of seam use a backstitch.

Place the pieces right sides together matching the edges and ends. Hold with long pins (page 23). Secure the start (page 50).

Backstitch along the seam one row or stitch from the edge. To backstitch bring the yarn from the back about ¼" from the end. Stitch back to the end and bring the needle up from the bottom, one stitch length in front of where the stitch started. Make the next stitches by stitching down through the beginning of the last stitch and forward two lengths.

Unusual Seams

Sometimes a seam does not work with either style of joining shown on pages 51 or 52.

As an example for joining these seams, bring the right edge together with the line formed when the stitching changes from a stockinette (rolled edge) to a body stitch pattern. Stitch with a ladder stitch along this line, leaving the rolled edge free.

Q. **How do I sew together ribbing?**

A. For ribbing with an odd number of double stitch ribs, use the ladder stitch, page 51. Stitch between the first and second stitches on each piece (as for a side edge). Each half will form a new double rib. You can use the ladder stitch for other ribbing seams although it may not make a perfect new rib.

stitch patterns

You can proceed to make the easy scarf on page 102 or use this opportunity to practice your knit and purl stitches. Using size 7 or 8 needles, cast on about 20 stitches in a medium (4)-weight yarn. Knit several rows, purl several rows and then practice ribbing and the seed or moss stitch (page 27).

When you are comfortable with this stitching, move on to work a few of the patterns on these pages. *These stitch patterns can also be found in the handy Stitch Patterns Summary (pages 114-115).* Cast on 2 or 3 multiples of the pattern. (If the pattern reads Multiple of 12 stitches; cast on 24 or 36.) Stitch 1 or 2 repeats of the rows until you are comfortable with the pattern. Keep this practice swatch for reference.

Argyle

Multiple of 10 stitches

Row 1 (right side): Knit 5, purl 1, knit 4; repeat these 10 stitches across the row.

Row 2: Purl 3, knit 1, purl 1, knit 1, purl 4; repeat these 10 stitches across the row.

Rows 3 and 7: Knit 3, purl 1, knit 3, purl 1, knit 2; repeat these 10 stitches across the rows.

Rows 4 and 6: Purl 1, knit 1, purl 5, knit 1, purl 1, knit 1; repeat these 10 stitches across the rows.

Row 5: Knit 1, purl 1, knit 3, purl 1, knit 3, purl 1; repeat these 10 stitches.

Row 8: Purl 3, knit 1, purl 1, knit 1, purl 4; repeat these 10 stitches.

Repeat these 8 rows.

Basket Weave

Multiple of 8 stitches

Rows 1 (right side) and 5: Knit all stitches across the row.

Rows 2 and 4: Knit 1, purl 3, knit 4; repeat these 8 stitches.

Row 3: Purl 5, knit 3; repeat these 8 stitches.

Rows 6 and 8: Knit 5, purl 3; repeat these 8 stitches.

Row 7: Purl 1, knit 3, purl 4; repeat these 8 stitches.

Repeat these 8 rows.

Zig Zag

Multiple of 12 stitches

Rows 1 (right side) and 2: Knit 6, purl 6; repeat these 12 stitches across the rows.

Row 3: Knit 10, purl 2; repeat these 12 stitches.

Row 4: Knit 2, purl 10; repeat these 12 stitches.

Rows 5 and 10: Purl 4, knit 6, purl 2; repeat these 12 stitches.

Rows 6 and 9: Knit 2, purl 6, knit 4; repeat these 12 stitches.

Row 7: Knit 2, purl 2, knit 8; repeat these 12 stitches.

Row 8: Purl 8, knit 2, purl 2; repeat these 12 stitches.

Row 11: Knit 6, purl 2, knit 4; repeat these 12 stitches.

Row 12: Purl 4, knit 2, purl 6; repeat these 12 stitches.

Repeat these 12 rows.

Ribbed Basket Weave

Multiple of 10 stitches

Rows 1 (right side), 3 and 5: Purl 5 (knit 1, purl 1) 2 times then knit 1; repeat these 10 stitches across the rows.

Rows 2, 4 and 6: (Purl 1, knit 1) 2 times then purl 6; repeat these 10 stitches.

Rows 7, 9 and 11: (Knit 1, purl 1) 2 times then knit 1, purl 5; repeat these 10 stitches.

Rows 8, 10 and 12: Purl 6 (knit 1, purl 1) 2 times; repeat these 10 stitches.

Repeat these 12 rows.

Reading a Pattern

If you've ever seen a knitting pattern, you know that knitting directions have a special type of shorthand. On the following pages, you'll find how to read abbreviations and symbols and how to understand color and stitch charts so you can follow knitting directions successfully and easily.

knitting abbreviations

approx	approximately
B	Back. The side of the knitting not facing while knitting a row or a round
beg	beginning
BO	bind off
C#B	C (cable), # (number of stitches in twist), B (back)
C#F	C (cable), # (number of stitches in twist), F (front)
CO	cast on
cn	cable needle
dec(s)	decrease(s)
dpn(s)	double-pointed needle(s)
inc(s)	increase(s)
k	knit
kb	knit into the back of the stitch
kf	knit into the front of a stitch
kf&b	knit into the front and back of a stitch (inc)
k2tog	knit 2 stitches together (dec)
kwise	insert needle as if to knit
m1	make 1 (inc)
m1p	make 1 purl (inc)
p	purl
patt	pattern
pm	place marker
psso	pass slipped stitch over
p2tog	purl 2 stitches together (dec)
pwise	insert needle as if to purl
RS	right side

rem	remaining
rep	repeat
rnd(s)	rounds
sk	skip
skp	slip one, knit 1, pass slip stitch over (dec)
sl	move stitch from left needle to right needle (Unless stated, this is a pwise slip.)
sm	slip marker
ssk	slip kwise, slip kwise, knit the slipped stitches together (dec)
st(s)	stitch(es)
St st	stockinette stitch (k 1 row, p 1 row)
tbl	through back of loop (work into back of stitch)
tog	together
WS	wrong side
wyib	with yarn in back
wyif	with yarn in front
yo	yarn over needle

knitting shorthand

* work instructions as directed from this point.

[ ] all instructions enclosed in brackets are to be worked as a group (work the number of times indicated).

( ) work instructions within parentheses where indicated and the number of times indicated.

— The number of stitches that should be on your needles or across a row is given after a dash at the end of the row. This serves as a checkpoint, especially after a section of increasing or decreasing.

Combining Abbreviations and Shorthand

The abbreviations and shorthand for knitting have been designed to reduce the length of knitting instructions and make them easier to read. Keep the Abbreviations near by, but as you progress, you will become accustomed to the lingo.

Most of the shorthand has to do with the repeating of stitches or a group of stitches. One common notation is the * (asterisk or star). Groups of stitches and instructions will be given after an *. This means you keep repeating this group of stitches inside the 2 asterisks. ***k1, p3, k4; rep from*** is an example from the basket weave pattern shown below. In the directions this group may have other directions before and/or after: **k4, *k1, p3, k4; rep from*, end k1**. In longhand, this means you knit 4 stitches, then for the rest of the row until you are 1 stitch from the end you will repeat the pattern of knit 1 stitch, purl 3 stitches, and knit 4 stitches.

This basket weave stitch pattern (Stitch Patterns 1) shows the use of a repeat between 2 asterisks.

Sometimes the instructions for a row have [ ] brackets and/or ( ) parentheses within the * (asterisk) repeat.
The following example from the ripple stitch pattern shown below ***(k2 tog) 2 times, [k1, yo] 4 times, (k2tog) 2 times; rep from* to end** uses both brackets and parentheses. In longhand, this means that you knit 2 stitches together twice, then repeat the pattern of knit 1 stitch, and yarn over 4 times, and then knit 2 stitches together twice. This whole sequence is then repeated to the end of the row. In the pattern instructions, this group may also have other directions before and/or after the brackets and/or parentheses.

This ripple stitch pattern (Stitch Patterns 4) shows the use of brackets and parentheses in a pattern row.

Pattern Multiples

When directions are talking about a stitch pattern (not the entire project) the number of stitches in one repeat will be specified as a multiple of X, or X plus Y. The pattern above would read: Multiple of 12 stitches. This means that the total number of stitches on the needle should be divisible by 12. The basket weave pattern at left would be a multiple of 8 + 5 or 13, 21 (16 + 5), 29 (24 + 5), etc.

reading charts

There are two types of charts in knitting instructions: a color chart and a stitch chart. They are frequently used to clarify instructions given in writing and sometimes they will be the only instructions.

Color Charts

A color chart tells you visually which color to use for each stitch. On a color chart, 1 square represents 1 stitch and 1 line of squares represents 1 row of knitting, unless otherwise indicated. Most charts are read from bottom to top, following numbered rows.

A color key will be given for each chart, detailing the colors represented and linking them by name to the materials list and other instructions. Sometimes a color chart will be given in black and white symbols rather than colors.

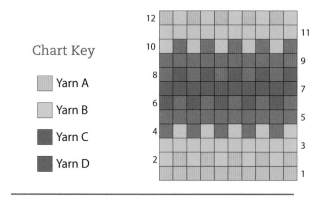

Chart Key

- Yarn A
- Yarn B
- Yarn C
- Yarn D

Stitch Charts

A stitch chart tells you with symbols which knitting stitch to work. In the chart, 1 square represents 1 stitch and 1 line of squares represents 1 row of knitting. Each square is filled with a symbol, sometimes including a blank square as a symbol.

Row 1 and all odd rows of the stitch chart are read from right to left. (This is because we knit the rows from right to left.) Row 2 and all even rows are read from left to right. Sometimes the even rows will be left out if they are a duplicate of the previous row or all knit or purl. All symbols indicate how the stitch would look on the right side of the project.

Stitch symbols are not universal. Any stitch chart will have a chart key indicating which symbol is used for a given stitch. For abbreviations refer to page 58.

Common chart symbols with abbreviations:

The chart below is for the Knotted Moss Stitch found on page 118 and Stitch Patterns 3. The repeat of the pattern is outlined in orange on the chart.

Knotted Moss Stitch

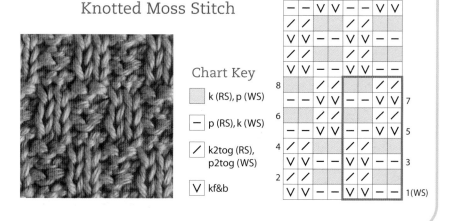

Chart Key

k (RS), p (WS)

− p (RS), k (WS)

／ k2tog (RS), p2tog (WS)

V kf&b

Going Beyond Basics

Now that you know how to knit and purl, you can go beyond to have fun with easy techniques that add texture and shape to your projects. Take the time to see what learning a few new techniques can do – from adding color and texture in a tote to embellishing with buttons and beads.

special stitches

There are several stitch techniques (knit or purl in back, yarn over and slip stitch) that are used alone or with other instructions.

Knit in Back (kb)

Basic knit and purl stitches are worked in the front of the loop, but sometimes the instructions will call for a knit or purl in the back of the stitch. This will give a twist to the stitch.

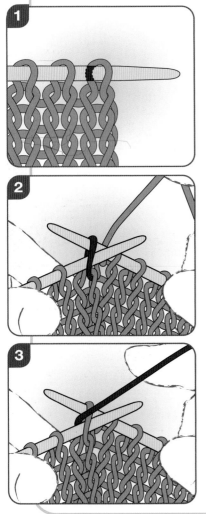

The back of the loop (behind the needle) is highlighted here in magenta.

To knit in back of the loop, insert the needle into the back of the stitch loop as shown.

Pass the yarn behind and then over the right needle. Then bring the tip of the right needle with the loop of yarn through the stitch as you would to complete a knit stitch.

The finished knit-in-back stitch will be twisted.

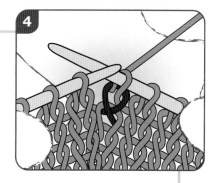

Purl in Back (pb)

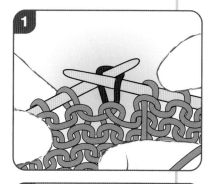

To purl in back of the loop, hold yarn in front and insert the needle into the back of the stitch loop, bringing it towards the front.

Pass the yarn around the right needle and between the needles from right to left. Then, move the tip of the right needle with the loop of yarn through the stitch and away from the front to complete the stitch.

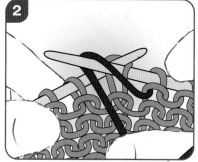

Q. Why do some instructions tell you to knit in front when that is the normal technique?

A. If knit in front is stated, it will usually be followed by another instruction to do immediately with the same stitch, ie., knit in front and in back (kf&b) of the stitch (page 74).

Yarn Over (yo)

A yarn over can be used to add extra length to a stitch, to give a lacy effect, or as a simple way to increase or add another stitch to a row.

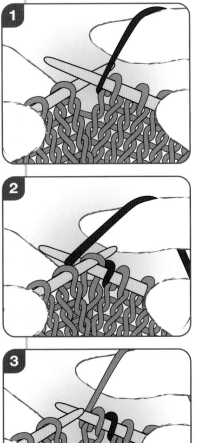

Yarn Over (Knitting)

If you are knitting, bring the yarn to the front.

Insert the right needle in the next stitch as to knit. Then pass the yarn behind and over the right needle. Complete the stitch.

Push the original stitch up and off the left needle.

Yarn Over (Purling)

If you are purling, begin with the yarn in front, wrap it around the right needle, and bring it back to the front.

Insert the right needle in the next stitch as to purl. Pass the yarn around the right needle and between the needles from right to left.

Complete the purl stitch, pushing the original stitch up and off the left needle.

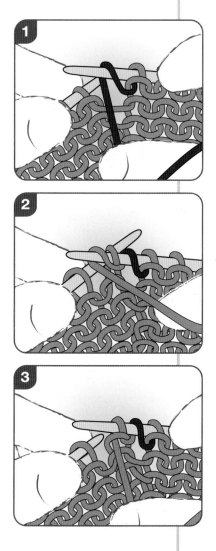

Slip Stitch (sl st)

A slip stitch is used in forming some patterns. Here are two ways to transfer a stitch from one needle to the other.

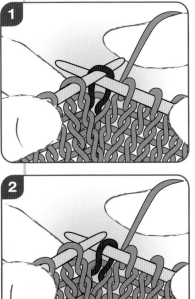

Knit-wise (sl st kwise)

To slip a stitch knit-wise, insert the right needle into the next stitch from left to right as you would to knit.

Slide the stitch off the left needle to the right needle.

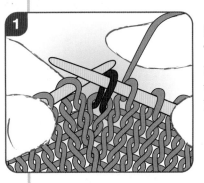

Purl-wise (sl st pwise)

To slip a stitch purl-wise, insert the right needle into the next stitch as you would to purl. Slide the stitch off the left needle to the right needle.

decrease

Decreasing adds shape and/or texture to a project. The decreases may be at the edge or in the middle of a row and when used with increases, are used to make pattern texture, rather than shape. There are several ways to decrease as you are knitting. Some types of decreases look different, so instructions may be specific about which type to use.

Knit Two Together (k2tog)

This is the quickest way to decrease. This type of decrease slants the finished stitch to the right.

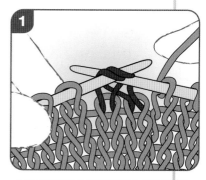

To knit two together, insert the right needle into the second stitch on the left needle and then into the first stitch.

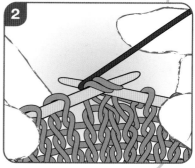

Pass the yarn behind and then over the right needle. Complete a knit stitch, pushing the original stitches up and off the left needle.

Purl Two Together (p2tog)

This is the quickest purl decrease. The finished stitch slants to the left on the purl side, but to the right on the knit side of a stockinette stitch.

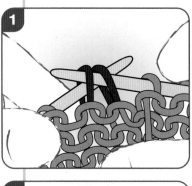

To purl two together, insert the right needle into the first stitch on the left needle and then into the second stitch.

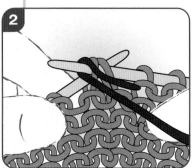

Pass the yarn around the right needle and between the needles from right to left and complete the purl stitch, pushing the original stitches up and off the left needle.

Q. **Why are some instructions specific about which type of decrease to use?**

A. Some decreases slant to the right and some to the left. If it is important to the look of the project, the designer will specify the type of decrease. If the decreases are on the very edge and do not show, it will not matter.

Slip, Slip, Knit (ssk)

This decrease slants the finished stitch to the left and will be called for, if that is important.

Using the right needle, slip the first stitch knit-wise (as if to knit, page 70).

Using the right needle, slip the second stitch knit-wise (as if to knit).

Insert the tip of the left needle into the slipped stitches on the right needle from left to right holding the stitches on both needles.

Pass the yarn behind and then over the right needle. Then complete a knit stitch, pushing the original stitches up and off the left needle.

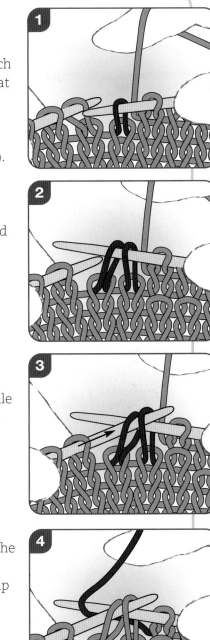

Slip, Knit, Pass Slipped Stitch Over (skp)

This decrease slants to the left and looks similar to ssk.
Practice both, use as directed, or choose the one you like best.

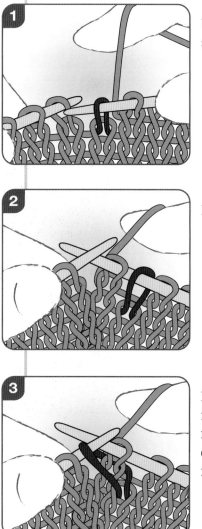

Using the right needle, slip the first stitch knit-wise (as if to knit, page 70).

Knit the next stitch to the right needle.

Insert the tip of the left needle into the front of the slipped stitch on the right needle from left to right. Lift this stitch over, the knit stitch and the tip of the right needle.

increase

Increasing adds shape and/or texture to knitting. Increases may be at the edge or in the middle of a row. When paired with decreases, they make pattern texture, rather than shape. Some types of increases look different, so instructions may be specific about which type to use. The increase happens in the row you are currently working. In the next row the new stitch is treated as any other stitch.

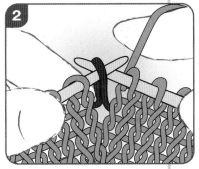

Make One (m1)

Created in the space between two stitches, make one is almost invisible.

Insert the left needle from front to back underneath the horizontal strand of thread between the two stitches and lift it up, creating a new stitch loop.

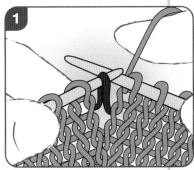

Insert the right needle in the back of this stitch loop. Proceed as for a knit stitch, wrapping and pulling the yarn through the just-made stitch loop.

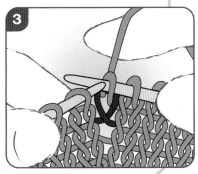

Slide the stitch loop off the left needle. The loop will be twisted.

If directed, bring the ball yarn to the front and purl in this stitch loop.

Bar Method (kf&b)

This increase creates a small bar where the increase is located and may not be the method of choice for some projects because the bar shows.

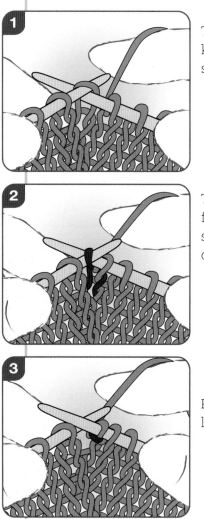

To increase (kf&b) in the next stitch, knit into the front (right side) of the stitch as you normally would.

Then, without removing the stitch from the left needle, make a knit stitch in the back (left side) of the original stitch.

Push the original stitch off the left needle.

Bar Method (pf&b)

If you are on a purl row or stitch and need to use this increase, purl in the front (right side) of the stitch, then without removing the stitch from the left needle, purl in the back (left side of the stitch). Push the original stitch off the left needle.

Backward Loop

The backward loop is a quick increase formed the same as a "loop E cast on" (page 34). It has the drawback that you must be careful not to drop it as you stitch in the next row. This increase is especially easy to use to add several stitches at the end or beginning of a row.

Using your left hand, make a backward loop of yarn around the right needle.

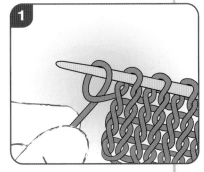

Pull the loop snug.

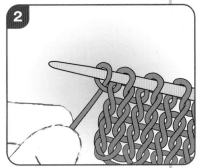

picking up stitches

Sometimes a pattern will call for picking up stitches along an already finished edge. This could be to add a neckline, a strap, or front facing.

Cast Off Edge

Hold the knitted piece in your left hand and with the right hand, insert a needle through the center of the first stitch just below the cast off ridge. Wrap a new length of yarn around the needle as if you were knitting. Using the needle tip, pull the new loop through the center of this stitch.

Continue inserting the needle through the center of each stitch, wrapping and pulling a loop through, across the row. You will be told the number of stitches to pick up. Frequently this is the same number of stitches as were on the cast off edge.

Vertical Edge

To pick up stitches from a vertical edge along the ends of the rows, hold the knitted piece in your left hand. Insert a needle in the space between the first two stitches. Wrap a new length of yarn around the needle as if to knit and pull a new loop through the space. Continue picking up the required number of stitches.

Diagonal Edge

To pick up stitches on a diagonal edge, work as for a cast-off edge or a vertical edge (page 78), inserting a needle in the first row between the first two stitches. Continue picking up the requested number of stitches spacing them evenly.

other techniques

Using Two Yarns

If you are using two or more colors of yarn and there are only a few rows separating the colors, you can twist them together instead of cutting and knotting each new color at the edge.

Twist the yarns together once or twice between rows and carry them up the side of the piece. Twist the opposite direction each time so you will not have to untangle your balls of yarn.

Using a Stitch Holder

Use a stitch holder to set aside stitches to be worked later. If a whole sweater or vest is started from the bottom, both of the fronts would be put on stitch holders while continuing to stitch the back.

Slip the number of stitches directed off the needle onto the stitch holder. When you are ready to knit, slip them onto the needle or knit directly off the stitch holder.

stitch patterns

Use this opportunity to practice some new stitching techniques. Using size 7 or 8 needles, cast on about 20 stitches in a medium (4)-weight yarn. Knit a few rows, then practice the special stitches, decreases, and increases on the preceding pages.

When you are comfortable with this stitching, work a few of the patterns on these pages. *These stitch patterns can also be found in the handy Stitch Patterns Summary (pages 116 - 117).* Cast on 2 or 3 multiples of the pattern. (If the pattern reads Multiple of 12 stitches; cast on 24 or 36.) Stitch 1 or 2 repeats of the rows. Keep these practice swatches for reference.

Textured Brick
Multiple of 4 + 2 stitches

Row 1 (RS): With Color #1, knit.
Row 2: Knit.
Row 3: With Color #2, k2 sl1, k3, repeat from * to end.
Row 4: Slip the previous sl st and purl all other st.
Row 5: With Color #1, knit.
Row 6: Knit
Row 7: With Color #3, k4 *sl1, k3, repeat from * to last 2 st, sl1, k1.
Row 8: Slip the previous sl st and purl all other st.
Repeat these 8 rows.

Chevron
Multiple of 21 stitches

Row 1 (RS): K2tog, yo, k2tog, k6, yo, k1, yo, k6, skp, yo, skp.
Row 2 : Purl
Repeat these 2 rows.

Knotted Moss
Multiple of 4 stitches

Rows 1 (WS) and 3: *P2, (kf&b) twice; repeat from * to end.
Rows 2 and 4: *(p2tog) 2 times, k2; repeat from * to end.
Rows 5 and 7: *(Kf&b) twice, p2; repeat from * to end.
Rows 6 and 8: *K2, (p2tog) 2 times; repeat from * to end.
Repeat these 8 rows.

Cable Eyelet
Multiple of 8 + 2 stitches

Row 1 (RS): P2, *k1, p2, sl1, k2, psso, p2; repeat from * to end.
Row 2: K2, *p1, yo, p1, k2, p1, k2; repeat from * to end.
Row 3: P2, *k1, p2, k3, p2; repeat from * to end.
Row 4: K2, *p3, k2, p1, k2; repeat from * to end.
Repeat these 4 rows.

Working with
Specialty
Needles

Many favorite fashions work up easily using specialty needles. A seamless sweater stays round on circular needles. Double-pointed needles make smaller tubes such as socks, mittens and caps. Cable stitches sit comfortably on cable needles. Be sure to read about the features and flexibility of these knitter-friendly needles. You'll enjoy using them.

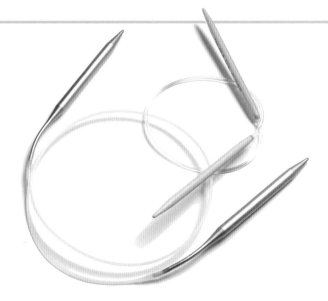

circular

Circular needles are short needles (about 6") that are connected by narrow, flexible nylon or plastic tubing. They can be used to knit a large seamless tube for a sweater or hat. Many times they are also used for large, flat projects or in place of straight needles where the knitting space may be confined.

Using Circular Needles

Use the specified length of circular needle. If the needle is too long, it will stretch the work. The needle should be a few inches smaller than the finished project. As you knit, keep moving stitches from the tubing up onto the left needle.

For a Tube

Cast on the directed number of stitches. Before joining the two ends, make sure there are no twists in the cast-on stitches. If instructed, place a marker on the right needle. As directed, knit or purl, the first stitch pulling the yarn, so there is no gap between these stitches.

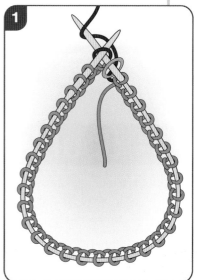

When you come to the place marker, slip it to the right needle and continue with your pattern. The marker will help keep track of each round you work.

After the first row, check again to make sure the work is not twisted. Continue knitting in the instructed pattern, creating a tube. The right side of the project will be around the outside of the tube.

Q. Why do some patterns call for circular needles when they are flat projects?

A. Because a circular needle is flexible and very thin in the middle, you can get a large number of stitches on it. Many projects would have too many stitches to fit on even the longest straight needles. Do not join ends as above, turn work as you would with straight needles.

double pointed

Double-pointed needles have points on both ends and come in a set of 4 or 5 matching needles. Use them to make small tubes, such as socks, mittens, and caps.

One needle of the double-pointed needle set is used as the empty right needle. A relatively equal number of stitches is put on each of the remaining needles. Work the stitches to the empty right needle. When all of the stitches have been worked off the current left needle, it becomes the next empty right needle. Continue working around the tube.

Illustrations 1 and 2 on the next page show a set of 4 double-pointed needles. The photo above and illustration 3 on the next page show a set of 5 double-pointed needles. The process of using them is the same. You may find that one or the other works best for you on a certain project.

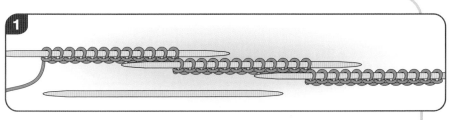

For a set of 4 double-pointed needles, cast on the directed number of stitches, putting an equal (or near equal) number on each of 3 needles.

Place the 3 needles in a triangle, making sure that the cast-on stitches are not twisted. If instructed, place a marker before the last cast on stitch. Insert one tip of the fourth needle into the first stitch and knit or purl, as directed, pulling the yarn so there is no gap between the first and last stitches.

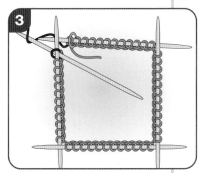

After the first row, check again to make sure the work is not twisted. Continue knitting as directed, creating a tube and slipping the marker. The right side of the project will be around the outside of the tube.

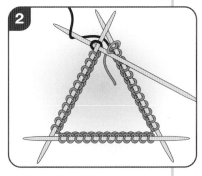

If you are using a set of 5 double-pointed needles, divide the stitches evenly between 4 needles and proceed as above with the fifth needle.

Q. How do you knit with the double-pointed needles?

A. Working the stitches on the left needle with the empty needle in your right hand, follow the stitch pattern. Center the stitches on the previous right needle and adjust it comfortably under your right hand so it is not in your way.

cable

Cable needles are short, curved double-pointed needles used to hold several stitches, either at the front or back of the work when creating a cable or twist pattern. They come in a variety of shapes and in metal or plastic. Placing the slipped stitches in front or back of the work will determine the direction of the cable twist.

Cable Shorthand Abbreviations

Knitting shorthand for using a cable needle includes all of the stitches involved in the twist. There are usually 3 parts to a cable instruction.

C directs that you are going to stitch a cable.

The number in the middle indicates how many stitches are involved in the whole cable unit.

F or **B** indicates whether the first half of the stitches is to be held in the front or back of the work.

For example: C4F means that 4 stitches are involved in the cable unit. Divide this number in half. The first 2 will be held to the front while knitting the other 2 stitches. **C6B** means that 6 stitches are involved in the cable unit. The first 3 will be held to the back while knitting the other 3 stitches.

Q. How do you cable with a U-shaped needle that has one longer side?

A. If the cable needle has one side longer than the other, slip the stitches onto the shorter end. Knit these stitches off from the long end.

Right-hand Cable (C6F)

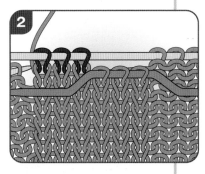

Slip 3 stitches onto the cable needle and hold in front of the work.

Knit the next 3 stitches onto the right needle.

Without twisting the cable needle, knit the stitches from it, working from right to left. Proceed with the rest of the row.

Left-hand Cable (C6B)

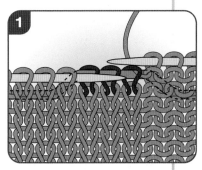

Slip 3 stitches onto the cable needle and hold in back of the work.

Knit the next 3 stitches from the left needle. Without twisting the cable needle, knit the stitches from the cable needle and proceed with the rest of the row.

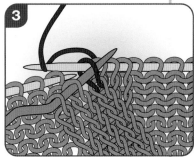

cable patterns

Now you have an opportunity to practice several cable patterns. Using size 7 or 8 needles, cast on about 20 stitches in a medium (4)-weight yarn. Knit several rows before you practice using the cable needle. The cable patterns here are stitched with 8 stockinette stitches on either side of the cable pattern. For all-over patterns, cast on 2 or 3 multiples of the pattern. (If the pattern reads Multiple of 12 stitches; cast on 24 or 36.) Work 1 or 2 repeats of the rows. Keep these practice swatches for reference. *These stitch patterns can also be found in the handy Stitch Patterns Summary (pages 121 - 125).*

Reflecting Cables
Multiple of 14
Two 6-stitch cables on reverse stockinette.

Rows 1 (RS) and 5: K6, p2, k6.
Rows 2 and 4: P6, k2, p6.
Row 3: C6B, p2, C6F.
Row 6: P6, k2, p6.
Repeat these 6 rows.

Mini Cables
Multiple of 10
Two 4-stitch cables on reverse stockinette.

Row 1 (RS): K4, p2, k4.
Row 2: P4, k2, p4.
Row 3: C4F, p2, C4B.
Row 4: P4, k2, p4.
Repeat these 4 rows.

Double Wave Cable
13-stitch cable on reverse stockinette.

Rows 1 (RS), 5, 7 and 11: K13.
Rows 2, 4, 6, 8 and 10: P13.
Row 3: C6B, k1, C6F.
Row 9: C6F, k1, C6B.
Row 12: P13.
Repeat these 12 rows.

Honeycomb
Multiple of 12 stitches.

Rows 1 (RS) and 5: K12.
Rows 2, 4 and 6: P12.
Row 3: *C4F, C4B; rep from * to end.
Row 7: *C4B, C4F; rep from * to end.
Row 8: P12.
Repeat these 8 rows.

Braided Cable
9-stitch braid on reverse stockinette.

Rows 1 (RS) and 5: K9.
Row 2 and all WS: P9.
Row 3: C6B, k3.
Row 7: K3, C6F.
Bow 8: P9.
Repeat these 8 rows.

Finishing
Touches

Fringes and tassels, buttons and beads add finishing touches and bring your projects to life.

On the following pages, learn how a no-hassle tassel finishes a scarf, or how to simply stitch on beads and buttons. Whether for convenience, funky fun or fashion, all it takes is a little know how and imagination to turn everyday into easy embellishments.

tassels

Tassels can be used to accent the top of a hat or the ends of a scarf.

Cut a 6" x 5" piece of corrugated cardboard . Wind desired yarn around the 6" length of the cardboard about 60 times, being careful not to get the yarn too tight and cause buckling of the board.

Slip a 16" length of yarn (shown here in rust) under the winding. Pull tightly and tie a double knot at the top.

Using scissors, cut through all of the winding at the opposite end of the board from the knot.

Cut a 36" length of yarn. Make a 4" loop of yarn at one end. Lay the yarn, loop end up on the cut tassel, about 1" from the top. Wind the remaining length of yarn snugly around the tassel to the desired thickness. Thread the remaining end of the yarn through the loop.

Pull on the wrapping end of the yarn to pull the loop under the winding. If necessary, trim the ends of tassel to make them even.

fringe

Decorate the ends of scarves and shawls with plain knotted fringe.

1 To make even lengths of yarn for fringe, wrap the yarn around a piece of cardboard that is a little larger than the finished length of fringe. Cut the yarn along one edge of the cardboard. Carefully set aside the yarn so it can be picked up in desired numbers to make the fringe.

2 Pick up the number of strands of fringe you want, fold them in half and hold in your left hand. Insert the crochet hook from back to front where you want to add the fringe near the edge. Place the fold of fringe in the hook.

3 Pull the crochet hook, tightening the fold of yarn in the hook and pull through to the under side.

Widen the newly formed loop and pull the yarn strands through. Pull to snug loop to knitting.

Fringe Extras

Special knots add more interest to the fringe.

To make knots between the fringes, divide the strands from each fringe in half. Tie an overhand knot (or square knot) with the strands of two adjoining fringes.

For interwoven knotting, divide the strands of each fringe in half and move the strands one space away in both directions from the original knot. Tie an overhand knot (or square knot) with the strands coming from 2 spaces away in the other direction.

Corner Tassels

This simple, uncut tassel is perfect on the no-hassle bulky knit Easy Scarf (page 102).

For an uncut tassel at the corner of a scarf, do not cut the wound yarn as for regular fringe. Slide the desired amount of

wound yarn off of the board. Fold in half and use a large crochet hook to pull the yarn through the corner. Widen the newly formed loop and pull the two ends through. Pull gently to snug loop to knitting.

Adding Beaded Fringe

Add instant interest with purchased beaded fringe.
Stitch ribbons of beaded fringe in place with strong matching

cotton sewing thread. For sequins (flat or textured disks with a hole in the center or edge) use matching cotton thread or nylon beading thread. If the hole is in the center of the sequin add a bead as an anchor.

Adding Beads

Before adding beads to a knitted garment, be sure the beads can be cleaned or washed along with the garment.

Stitch beads to the knitting, using matching sewing thread or nylon beading thread. Make a few back stitches or a knot every several beads, so if the thread breaks, you will not lose all of the beads.

Adding Buttons

Because knitting is frequently soft and loose, it is good to stabilize the area where you are going to add a button.

Place a matching piece of felt, leather, or non-woven interfacing on the wrong side of the knitted piece for stabilizer. Sew the button on through both the knitting and the stabilizer. Use the knitting yarn or strong matching sewing thread to sew on the button.

lining a purse

Because of its flexible structure, most knit purses and bags need to be lined.

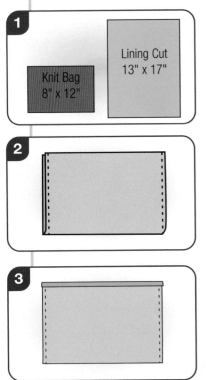

1 Knit Bag 8" x 12" | Lining Cut 13" x 17"

Make a purse lining from sturdy cotton or synthetic lining fabric. Measure the bag and cut a lining piece the width of the bag X twice the length of the bag plus 1" in both directions.

2 Fold the lining right sides together and stitch ½"-wide side seams.

3 At the top opening, fold under a ½" seam allowance to the wrong side.

Insert into bag and pin in place about ½" from the top edge. Hand stitch lining to purse.

Adding extra pockets

If you want extra pockets, as this one for a cell phone, stitch them to the lining before sewing into the bag. Fabric can also be stitched to the handle for added stability.

projects

stitch patterns

easy scarf
Designed by Janet Pittman

Finished Size: 6.5" x 84"

easy scarf

Materials

Yarn:

SUPER BULKY

This Project:
Di.Vé®, Fiamma
100% wool
1¾ oz skein/55 yds
5 skeins #35329 multi-colored

Needles:
Size 13 (5mm) straight needles

Adjust needle size to obtain correct gauge.

Notions:
Measuring tape, tapestry needle, crochet hook

Gauge
12 stitches = 4" in stockinette stitch (pg. 26)
3 stitches = 1"

Scarf Directions

Cast on 20 stitches.

Row 1 and all other rows: Knit all stitches.

Referring to page 44, add a new ball of yarn when necessary.

Knit until scarf measures about 84" long.

Bind off.

Finishing

1. Weave in yarn ends (page 44).

2. For each corner tassel, refer to directions on page 94 and wind yarn around an 8" piece of corrugated board or cardboard nine times. Slip yarn off the board without cutting. Using a large crochet hook, attach to corner of scarf (page 98).

Techniques
Add new yarn	Knit
Bind off	Weave in ends
Cast on	

winter warmers

Designed by Joyce Nordstrom

winter warmers

Materials

Yarn:

MEDIUM

This Project:
Red Heart Yarn, Strata
100% Acrylic
4 oz skein/202yd
1 skein #8569 Splash

Needles:
Size 7 (4½ mm)
double-pointed
needles
*Adjust needle size to
obtain correct gauge.*

Notions:
Measuring tape,
tapestry needle

Gauge
28 stitches = 4" in
ribbing pattern (pg. 27)
7 stitches = 1"

Hand Warmer Directions

With size 7 double-pointed needles, cast on 40 (44, 48) sts.

Divide sts evenly on 3 or 4 needles and join, being careful not to twist sts. Add pm at beg of round.

Work in k2, p2 (ribbing) for 6.5" (7", 8") or desired length from V of thumb.

Bind off 6 (6, 8) sts; complete row in ribbing.

Cast on 2 (2, 4) sts over bound off sts and continue around row.

Work in k2, p2 (ribbing) for 2".

Bind off.

Repeat for second Hand Warmer.

Finishing

Weave in yarn ends (page 44).

Techniques

Chapter 2:
  Add new yarn
  Bind off
  Cast on
  Knit

Purl
Weave in ends
Chapter 5:
  Double-pointed
  needles

Abbreviations

k–knit
p–purl
pm–place marker
RS–right side
rem–remaining
st(s)–stitch(es)

ribbed cable cap

Designed by Joyce Nordstrom

INTERMEDIATE

ribbed cable cap

Materials

Yarn:

MEDIUM

This Project:
Red Heart Super Saver®
100% Acrylic
3 oz skein/160 yds
1 skein #378 Claret

Needles:
Size 6 (4mm) and size 8
(5mm)16" circular
needles 8 (5mm), double
pointed needles
*Adjust needle size to
obtain correct gauge.*

Notions:
Measuring tape, place
markers, tapestry needle

Gauge
16 stitches = 4" in
stockinette stitch (pg. 26)
4 stitches = 1"

Stitch Patterns

Beaded Ribbing (BR)
(multiple of 5 sts)

Row 1: Knit.

Row 2: (P1, k1) twice, p1.

Little Cable (LC)
(multiple of 4 sts)

Row 1: P1, k2, p1.

Row 2: P1, (sk 1 st, k into 2nd st, knit
into skipped stitch, drop both sts from
left needle), p1.

Hat Directions

With size 6 circular needle, cast on 86
stitches.

Work (k1, p1) ribbing across. Taking
care not to twist row, join to beg of row.

Techniques

Chapter 2:	Place markers	Chapter 5:
Bind off	Weave in ends	Circular needles
Cast on	Chapter 4:	Double-pointed
Knit	Decrease	needles
Purl	Slip	

ribbed cable cap

Work in k1, p1 ribbing until ribbing measures 4", k2tog 1 time on last row – 85 sts. Add pm after last stitch.

Change to size 8 needle.

Row 1 (RS): *K13 (includes Row 1 of BR), add different colored pm, [p1, k2, p1] for LC, add pm; rep from * 4 times – 5 LC.

Row 2: Sm here and throughout, *k4, Row 2 of BR, k4, Row 2 of LC; rep from * 4 times.

Work as established, working LC and BR Rows 1 and 2 as set up and sm until piece measures 9" from beg, ending with Row 2.

Shape Crown:
Change to size 8 double-pointed needles.

Row 1: (Sm, k2tog, work to 2 sts before next marker, ssk, sm, LC over next 4 sts) 5 times – 75 sts.

Row 2: Sm, work 1 row even in patt.

Repeat Rows 1 and 2, maintaining LC and BR until 1 st rem between markers – 25 sts.

Abbreviations

beg–beginning	rem–remaining
dec–decrease	rep–repeat
k–knit	sk–skip
k2tog–knit 2 together	sm–slip marker
p–purl	ssk–slip, slip, knit
patt–pattern	st(s)–stitch(es)
pm–place marker	WS–wrong side
RS–right side	

Cut yarn, leaving a 12" strand for top of hat. Thread yarn through tapestry needle, weave through rem sts & pull up tightly; secure. Fasten off.

Knit I-cord:

With size 6 circular needle, cast on 3 stitches.

Row 1: Slide sts to the other end of the needle. This point is now the left needle. Insert the right point into the first st; pull the yarn connected to the left side of the sts across the back and use as the working yarn. Knit the 3 sts.

Row 2: Slide sts to the other end of the needle and rep Row 1.

Repeat these rows until I-cord measures about 7".

Bind off.

Finishing

1. Weave in yarn ends (page 44).

frequently asked questions

Q. How do I know if I have enough yarn to knit another row?

A. You will need a length about 3 times the width of the row.

Q. How do I cast on at the beginning of a row?

A. Refer to page 34 for the Loop Cast On method. This can be done at the end or the beginning of a row.

Q. Is there a different way for left-handers to knit?

A. Because knitting involves the use of both hands, most left-handers do not feel the need to knit a different way. Even right-handed beginners have to learn how to coordinate the opposite hand.

Q. How often do I need to count the stitches in a row?

A. When you are just starting out or are working on a new stitch pattern, it is good to count the stitches for several rows to make sure you have not added or dropped some stitches.

Q. Should all my stitches look the same on the needle?

A. Yes, all stitches, whether they have been knit or purled on the previous row should be looped over the left needle in the same direction. The right side of the loop will be in front of and the left side of the loop will be behind the needle.

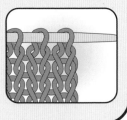

Q. My ribbing pattern calls for "knit the knit stitches" and "purl the purl stitches". What does this mean?

A. This means to make a stitch that looks just like the one under it. So, if the stitch has the loop coming toward you, purl the stitch. If the loop is on the reverse side, knit the stitch.

Q. What does it mean to increase (or decrease) 6 stitches evenly spaced across the row?

A. This instruction is usually given after a ribbed border to add extra width to the body of the project. You can visually estimate the 7 divisions across the work or actually divide the number of stitches and count them. Mark the points for increase with place markers that open or safety pins. Stitch across, slipping off the markers and make the increases.

Q. What if you do not have a stitch holder?

A. For a few stitches you can use a large safety pin or a U-shaped cable needle. For a lot of stitches you can use a circular needle (page 20) or a strand of yarn.

Q. What does "work in established pattern" mean?

A. This means to keep the stitch pattern(s) going as you work across the rows even while following other instructions. These instructions may be to decrease as in the photo at right.

Q. What if my circular knitting gets twisted when I join the ends?

A. If you have only gone a row or two, untwist the worked rows at the beginning of the next round and continue knitting. There will be a small twist at the bottom of the piece. If you have gone more than two rows you will probably need to unravel and start over.

Q. How can I manage the extra needle when working with double-pointed needles?

A. Start with the new needle in front of the last working needle for a knit stitch and behind the last working needle for a purl stitch.

Q. What if I don't have a cable needle?

A. You can use a double-pointed or circular needle in place of a cable needle, or, in desperation, use an unfolded large paper clip.

Q. How do I make stripes match with variegated yarn?

A. When using Strata yarn or other yarns made with distinct, regular color changes (like the hand warmers at right), consider starting each piece at the same point in the yarn-color pattern.

Stitch
Patterns

- Argyle
- Ribbed Basket Weave
- Basket Weave
- Zig Zag
- Twisted Ribbing
- Chevron
- Bamboo Rib
- Ribbed Seed Stitch
- Knotted Moss
- Cable Eyelet
- Textured Brick
- Ribbed Eyelet
- Feathered Eyelet
- Ripples
- Easy Shell
- Honeycomb
- Hat Stitch Pattern
- On Point Eyelet
- Mini Cables
- Mosaic
- Reflecting Cables
- Braided Cable
- Double Wave Cable
- Single Wave Cable

stitch patterns 1

Argyle

Multiple of 10 stitches

Row 1 (RS): *K5, p1, k4; rep from * to end.
Row 2: *P3, k1, p1, k1, p4; rep from * to end.
Rows 3 and 7: *K3, p1, k3, p1, k2; rep from * to end.
Rows 4 and 6: *P1, k1, p5, k1, p1, k1; rep from * to end.
Row 5: *K1, p1, k3, p1, k3, p1; rep from * to end.
Row 8: *P3, k1, p1, k1, p4; rep from * to end.
Repeat these 8 rows.

Ribbed Basket Weave

Multiple of 10 stitches

Rows 1 (RS), 3 and 5: *P5, (k1, pk1) 2 times, k1; rep from * to end.
Rows 2, 4 and 6: *(P1, k1) 2 times, p6; rep from * to end.
Rows 7, 9 and 11: *(K1, p1) 2 times, k1, p5; rep from * to end.
Rows 8, 10 and 12: *P6, (k1, p1) 2 times; rep from * to end.
Repeat these 12 rows.

Basket Weave

Multiple of 8 stitches

Rows 1 (RS) and 5: Knit.
Rows 2 and 4: *K1, p3, k4; rep from *
to end.
Row 3: *P5, k3; rep from * to end.
Rows 6 and 8: *K5, p3; rep from * to end.
Row 7: *P1, k3, p4; rep from * to end.
Repeat these 8 rows.

Zig Zag

Multiple of 12 stitches

Rows 1 (RS) and 2: *K6, p 6; rep from *
to end.
Row 3: *K10, p2; rep from * to end.
Row 4: *K2, p10; rep from * to end.
Rows 5 and 10: *P4, k6, p2; rep from *
to end.
Rows 6 and 9: *K2, p6, k4; rep from *
to end.
Row 7: *K2, p2, k8; rep from * to end.
Row 8: *P8, k2, p2; rep from * to end.
Row 11: *K6, p2, k4; rep from * to end.
Row 12: *P4, k2, p6; rep from * to end.
Repeat these 12 rows.

Twisted Ribbing

Multiple of 8 stitches

Row 1 (RS): Sl1pwise (k1, k1b) 3 times, k1.
Row 2: Purl.
Repeat these 2 rows.

Chevron

Multiple of 21 stitches

Row 1 (RS): K2tog, yo, k2tog, k6, yo, k1, yo, k6, skp, yo, skp.
Row 2: Purl.
Repeat these 2 rows.

Bamboo Rib

Multiple of 10 stitches

Rows 1 (RS), 3, 5 and 7: *K3, p2; rep from * to end.
Rows 2 and 6: *K2, p3; rep from * to end.
Row 4: *K2, p3, k7; rep from * to last 8 st, p3, k5.
Row 8: *K7, p3; rep from * to end.
Repeat these 8 rows.

Ribbed Seed Stitch

Multiple of 10 stitches

Row 1(RS): *(K1, p1) 3 times, k4; rep from * to end.
Row 2: *P4, (p1, k1) 3 times; rep from * to end.
Repeat these 2 rows.

stitch patterns 3

Knotted Moss

Multiple of 4 stitches

Rows 1 (WS) and 3: *P2, (kf&b) twice; repeat from * to end.
Rows 2 and 4: *(P2tog) 2 times, k2; repeat from * to end.
Rows 5 and 7: *(Kf&b) twice, p2; repeat from * to end.
Rows 6 and 8: *K2, (p2tog) 2 times; repeat from * to end.
Repeat these 8 rows.

Cable Eyelet

Multiple of 8 + 2 stitches

Row 1 (RS): P2, *k1, p2, sl1, k2, psso, p2; repeat from * to end.
Row 2: K2, *p1, yo, p1, k2, p1, k2; repeat from * to end.
Row 3: P2, *k1, p2, k3, p2; repeat from * to end.
Row 4: K2, *p3, k2, p1, k2; repeat from * to end.
Repeat these 4 rows.

Textured Brick

Multiple of 4 + 2 stitches

Row 1 (RS): With Color 1, knit.
Row 2: Knit.
Row 3: With Color 2, k2 *sl1, k3, repeat from * to end.
Row 4: Slip the previous sl st and purl all other sts.
Row 5: With Color 1, knit.
Row 6: Knit.
Row 7: With Color 3, k4 *sl1, k3, repeat from * to last 2 st, sl1, k1.
Row 8: Slip the previous sl st and purl all other sts.
Repeat these 8 rows.

Ribbed Eyelet

Multiple of 9 + 3 stitches

Row 1 (RS): *K3, p2, yo, ssk, p2; repeat from *, end k3.
Rows 2 and 4: *P3, k2, p2, k2; repeat from *, end p3.
Row 3: *K3, p2, k2tog, yo, p2; repeat from *, end k3.
Repeat these 4 rows.

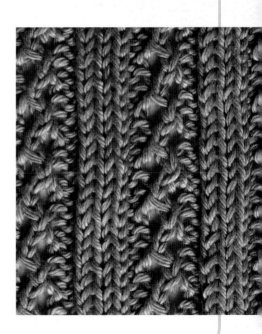

stitch patterns 4

Feathered Eyelet

Multiple of 7 stitches

Row 1 (RS): *K2, k2tog, yo, k3; repeat from * to end.
Rows 2, 4, 6: Purl.
Row 3: *K1, k2tog, yo, k4; repeat from * to end.
Row 5: *K2, yo, ssk, k3; repeat from * to end.
Row 7: *K4, yo, ssk, k1; repeat from * to end.
Row 8: Purl.
Repeat these 8 rows.

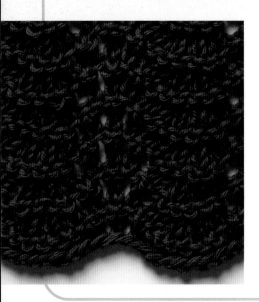

Ripples

Multiple of 12 stitches

Row 1 (RS): *(K2tog) 2 times, (k1,yo) 4 times, (k2tog) 2 times repeat from * to end.
Rows 2 and 3: Knit.
Row 4: Purl.
Repeat these 4 rows.

Easy Shell

Multiple of 7 + 2 stitches

Row 1 (RS): Knit.
Row 2: Purl.
Row 3: K2, *yo, p1, p3tog, p1, yo, k2; rep from * to end.
Row 4: Purl.
Repeat these 4 rows.

Honeycomb

Multiple of 12 stitches

Rows 1 (RS) and 5: K12.
Rows 2, 4, and 6: P12.
Row 3: *C4F, C4B; rep from * to end.
Row 7: *C4B, C4F; rep from * to end.
Row 8: P12.
Repeat these 8 rows.

stitch patterns 5

Hat Stitch Pattern

Multiple of 9 stitches

Row 1 (WS): *K5, p1, k2, p1; rep from * to end.
Row 2 (RS): *P1, (sk 1 st, k into 2nd st, knit into skipped stitch, drop both sts from left needle), p2, k1, p1, k1, p1; rep from * to end.
Repeat these 2 rows.

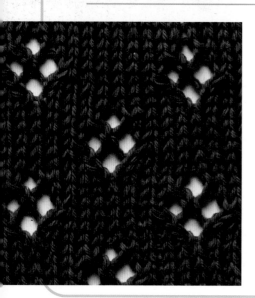

On Point Eyelet

Multiple of 10 stitches

Row 1 (RS): Knit.
Row 2 and all even rows: Purl.
Rows 3 and 7: *K2, yo, skp, k6; rep from * to end.
Row 5: *K2tog, yo, k1, yo, skp, k5; rep from * to end.
Rows 9 and 13: *K7, yo, skp, k1; rep from * to end.
Row 11: *K5, k2tog, yo, k1, yo, skp; rep from * to end.
Row 14: Purl.
Repeat Rows 3 through 14.

Mini Cables

Multiple of 10
Two 4-stitch cables on reverse
stockinette stitch.

Row 1 (RS): K4, p2, k4.
Row 2: P4, k2, p4.
Row 3: C4F, p2, C4B.
Row 4: P4, k2, p4.
Repeat these 4 rows.

Mosaic

Multiple of 10 + 3. Change color every 2 rows.
Rows 1 and 2: Knit all sts.
Row 3: K1, *sl wyib, k9; rep from *, to last 2 sts, sl wyib, k1.
Row 4: K1, *sl wyif, k9; rep from *, to last 2 sts, sl wyif, k1.
Row 5: K1, *k1, sl wyib, k7, sl wyib; rep from *, to last 2 sts, k2.
Row 6: K1, *k1, sl wyif, k7, sl wyif; rep from *, to last 2 sts, k2.
Row 7: K1, *k2, sl wyib, k5, sl wyib, k1; rep from *, to last 2 sts, k2.
Row 8: K1, *k2, sl wyif, k5, sl wyif, k1; rep from *, to last 2 sts, k2.
Row 9: K1, *k3, sl wyib, k3, sl wyib, k2; rep from *, to last 2 sts, k2.
Row 10: K1, *k3, sl wyif, k3, sl wyif, k2; rep from *, to last 2 sts, k2.
Row 11: K1, *k4, sl wyib, k1, sl wyib, k3; rep from *, to last 2 sts, k2.
Row 12: K1, *k4, sl wyif, k1, sl wyif, k3; rep from *, to last 2 sts, k2.
Row 13: K1, *k5, sl wyib, k4; rep from *, to last 2 sts, k2.
Row 14: K1, *k5, sl wyif, k4; rep from *, to last 2 sts, k2.
Repeat these 14 rows using 1 new color and 1 repeat color.

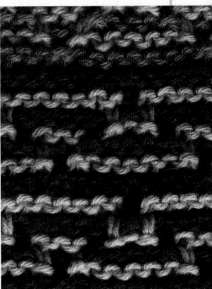

stitch patterns 6

Reflecting Cables

Multiple of 14
Two 6-stitch cables on reverse stockinette stitch.

Rows 1 (RS), and 5: K6, p2, k6.
Rows 2 and 4: P6, k2, p6.
Row 3: C6B, p2, C6F.
Row 6: P6, k2, p6.
Repeat these 6 rows.

Braided Cable

9-stitch braid on reverse stockinette stitch.

Rows 1 (RS) and 5: Knit 9.
Row 2 and all WS rows: Purl 9.
Row 3: C6B, knit 3.
Row 7: Knit 3, C6F.
Bow 8: Purl 9.
Repeat these 8 rows.

Double Wave Cable

13-stitch cable on reverse stockinette stitch.

Rows 1 (RS), 5, 7 and 11: K13.
Rows 2, 4, 6, 8 and 10: P 13.
Row 3: C6B, k1, C6F.
Row 9: C6F, k1, C6B.
Row 12: P13.
Repeat these 12 rows.

Single Wave Cable

8-stitch cable with echo on reverse stockinette stitch.

Rows 1 (RS), 5, 7, 9, 13 and 15: K1, p1, k8, p1, k1.
Rows 2, 4, 6, 8, 10, 12 and 14: P1, k1, p8, k1, p1.
Row 3: K1, p1, C8B, p1, k1.
Row 11: K1, p1, C8F, p1, k1.
Row 16: K1, p1, k8, p1, k1.
Repeat these 16 rows.

index